The Prayer of Repentance —
dictated by Meher Baba, November 1951

We repent, O God most merciful, for all our sins; for every thought that was false or unjust or unclean; for every word spoken that ought not to have been spoken; for every deed done that ought not to have been done.

We repent for every deed and word and thought inspired by selfishness; and for every deed and word and thought inspired by hatred.

We repent most specially for every lustful thought and every lustful action; for every lie; for all hypocrisy; for every promise given but not fulfilled; and for all slander and backbiting.

Most specially also, we repent for every action that has brought ruin to others; for every word and deed that has given others pain; and for every wish that pain should befall others.

In Your unbounded mercy, we ask You to forgive us, O God, for all these sins committed by us, and to forgive us for our constant failures to think and speak and act according to Your Will.

Dedicated to Beloved Avatar Meher Baba

BEFORE

Heartland Pilgrimage 2013: Official Statement of Purpose — Jill

The purpose of this pilgrimage is to endeavor to experience and creatively express the oneness that lies at the heart of all. This journey will include sites along the Cherokee Trail of Tears, Meher Baba's car 'accident' in Prague, Oklahoma, and sites significant to the Freedom Riders of the American civil rights movement. The intention of this pilgrimage is to recognize our shared human experience and explore the meaning of forgiveness. We will offer prayers of repentance for violations of human dignity, and ask for an awakening to the reality of the One in all. Through companionship, intuitive guidance and the journey itself, we hope to galvanize a deeper sense of personal connection to the one truth which binds all creation.

Companions on the 2013 Heartland Beads-on-One-String Pilgrimage:

Richard F. Budd	East Sussex, UK
Dhiresha (Dee) Chapman	Thirroul, NSW, AU
Lois Colton	Hood River, OR
Carole Cunningham	Arcadia, CA
Jill English	Westminster, CO
Don Eucker	Cedar Grove, NJ
Margaret Eucker	Cedar Grove, NJ
Cheryl Garnant	N. Myrtle Beach, SC
Kathryn Harris	Englewood, CO
Kiva Harris	Englewood, CO
Karl Moeller	Tucson, AZ
Anisa Shah	Lakewood, CO
Danielle Shah	Lakewood, CO
Irma Sheppard	Tucson, AZ
Robin Slemenda	Silverton, OR

Dedication: Heartland Pilgrimage

My work in designing the structure of the Heartland 2013 itinerary is due to the love and inspiration of my life, Don E. Stevens. Magical synchronization in the chain of resources manifested as I pored over each step of these painful acts of American history.

None of this could have been experienced except for the vision of the Beads-on-One-String Board of Directors, who felt the depth and importance of the idea, expressing their loving support, which is, in my opinion, Meher Baba giving His characteristic 'OK' sign of approval to my efforts. Because Don was so often tangibly by my side, standing next to my right shoulder, seemingly guiding my thoughts and intuitions, how could it be otherwise? Don was Baba's 'boy' after all.

It is my great privilege to be the catalyst, albeit somewhat unwitting, for these efforts coming to 'reality.' For this incredible blessing I dedicate every ounce of my work to the memory of my beloved Don, to his legacy of genuine love for humanity, his insight into life, discipline and indefatigable service to preserving Meher Baba's words; but most specially for his expressed wish to move us into action by exploring the delivery of spiritual charge as agents for Baba's 'beads on one string' intention.

It is real, purposeful work, which includes the inherent gift of actively striving toward unity in a broader realm outside of our familiar communities. By seeking forgiveness on behalf of our ancestors from peoples who have been recipients of their greed, ignorance and hate, causing generational grief and trauma, we begin to heal ourselves and our own ancestors. The implication of this holds much to contemplate personally and globally. It is no small thing, though we must take baby steps, possibly over lifetimes, to create an effect. These steps seek to create a strong, conscious, inner link with humanity, so real unity is discovered and experienced as truth. This is the legacy left to us as the truth of being part of creation.

To Be A Pilgrim

To Be A Pilgrim
He who would valiant be
'Gainst all disaster
Let him in constancy
Follow the master.
There's no discouragement
Shall make him once relent
His first avowed intent
To be a pilgrim

—hymn by John Bunyan

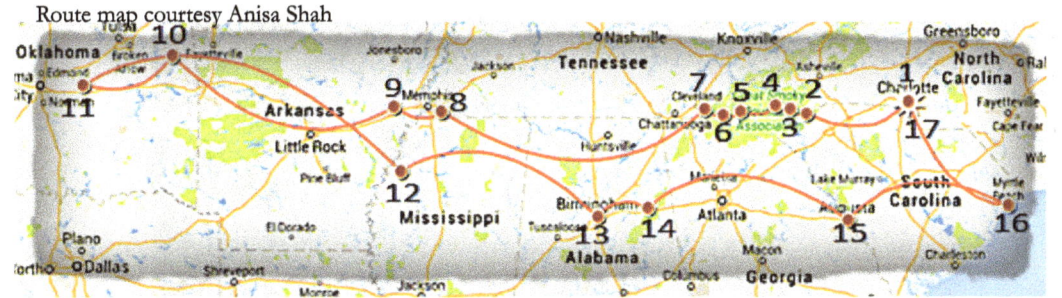

Route map courtesy Anisa Shah

State Abbreviations Used:

NC - North Carolina
SC - South Carolina
TN - Tennessee
GA - Georgia
AL - Alabama
MS - Mississippi
AR - Arkansas
OK - Oklahoma

Robin's Dream — September 9, 2013

I am working in an acupuncture clinic and feeling inept, as when I volunteered to work in Goher's clinic on my first trip to India in 1985. I am given the task of inserting a metal sheath into all of the patients' backs for the Doctor to be able to easily slide the needle in. I have to push the sharp, arrow-shaped sheath in just to the right of the left scapula. An incredible mix of people is present for treatment—I especially remember Buddhist monks in beautiful gold-colored robes. Dr. Silva is there though I do not interact with her. I cannot understand why I am there doing this work, yet I know I have to. I insert one more shaft. Then Baba comes into the dream and moves in to treat the patient. He is standing at the foot of the treatment table *but it feels like He is almost standing over the patient. Baba is the needle. He enters the person. It's like a translucent piece of Baba peels off, lies over the person and goes into the shaft.* Baba tells me I must continue to help insert these arrows so He can enter our hearts, keep them open and full of Him. He appears as the Beloved of the late forties, early fifties—so beautiful and flowing.

DURING

Richard:

The Trail of Tears tour is for me one not of Forgiveness but of Oneness.

Carole:

We are fifteen Baba lovers traveling in two vans, many of us unknown to each other: three men and twelve women, ranging in age from thirteen to eighty-one; two married couples one mother-daughter team and one grandmother-mother-granddaughter team; the rest are single adults.

```
                    ITINERARY
Day 1 Sep 23 Monday  265 MI
• Charlotte, NC to Caesar's Head
• to Silver Run Falls for lunch and water ceremony with
  Lianna Constantino of the Cherokee tribe
• to Niquasi Mound in Franklin, TN, meet Carol Long of the
  Cherokee tribe Coalition of Healing and Wellness
• to Ducktown, TN
Day 2 Sep 24 Tuesday 397 MI
• to Nancy Ward gravesite with Lianna and Carol
• to Germantown, TN, sleep
Day 3 Sep 25 Wednesday  396 MI
• to Village Creek State Park, visitors' center, land
  bridge, river
• to Talequah, OK, traditional village welcome dance and
  sing, sang Amazing Grace in Cherokee, met Ryan (Wah'de)
  Mackey and others, to Sam and Ella's for pizza
Day 4 Sep 26 Thursday  671 MI
• to Prague, OK, AMB crash site, to Heartland Center, lunch
• turn around, head EAST
• to Clarksdale, MI, meet Catherine Burks-Brooks, take her
  to Zero Point Blues Club for dinner
Day 5 Sep 27 Friday 408 MI
• to Yazoo Pass, MI, Parchman State Penitentiary with
  Catherine Burks-Brooks
• to Yazoo Pass for lunch
• Dinner with Catherine Burks-Brooks
• to Birmingham, AL
Day 6 Sep 28 Saturday  151 MI
• Birmingham, AL to 16th Street Baptist Church, Civil
  Rights Museum
• to Anniston, AL to former Greyhound Station at 1031
  Gurnee Ave, met Freedom Rider Georgia Calhoun and EPIC
  Director Pete Conroy
• to Wall of Hope, lunch, Bus Burning site, future Freedom
  Rider Park with 32nd District State Representative
  Barbara Boyd
• Dinner at Anniston's 'Classic On Noble' restaurant
• to Atlanta, GA
Day 7 Sep 29 Sunday 370 MI
• to Myrtle Beach, SC

total approx 2658 miles not including U-turns and
backtracking
```

These two quotes from Meher Baba came to mind often during our Pilgrimage:

"Give in for the sake of harmony. I do not mind crises, I do not mind chaos, but I do mind disharmony."

"It is easier to go through fire than to give in. It is a more difficult task than creating the creation, to turn a selfish person into an unselfish one, to turn stubbornness into flexibility!"

One mission of our pilgrimage was to ask forgiveness from those who had been wronged and harmed along each of these routes. We invited our ancestral fathers and mothers to be with us as we read two prayers of repentance. Everyone we encountered had experienced a religion other than their own being forced on them. In silence, Avatar Meher Baba was with us every step and word of the way.

Day 1- September 23 — Charlotte, NC

Lois:

We traveled on twisty, two-lane roads, in and out of the heavily forested mountains of North and South Carolina. At the end of the first day, I wrote: "We are sleeping tonight in Ducktown, TN, a small mountain resort and mining town named for a Cherokee chief whose name translates into the English word 'duck.'"

Caesar's Head, NC gave us a view into the misty Blue Ridge Mountains. Formerly called Chieftain's Head, a sacred spot to the Cherokee, it was one of the places Baba and the women mandali had stopped to picnic on their fateful road trip from east to west in May of 1952. We considered this the beginning of our pilgrimage and initiated our journey by reciting the prayers and poems for the first time. We acknowledged we were now in what had once been the vast Cherokee homelands, and that we would be continuing west along the route of the Trail of Tears as Baba had before us. In the 1830s thousands of American Indians from Southeastern tribes had been banished from their ancient homelands and force-marched into Oklahoma Territory, a long-suffering journey referred to as the Trail of Tears.

Looking out from Caesar's Head South Carolina

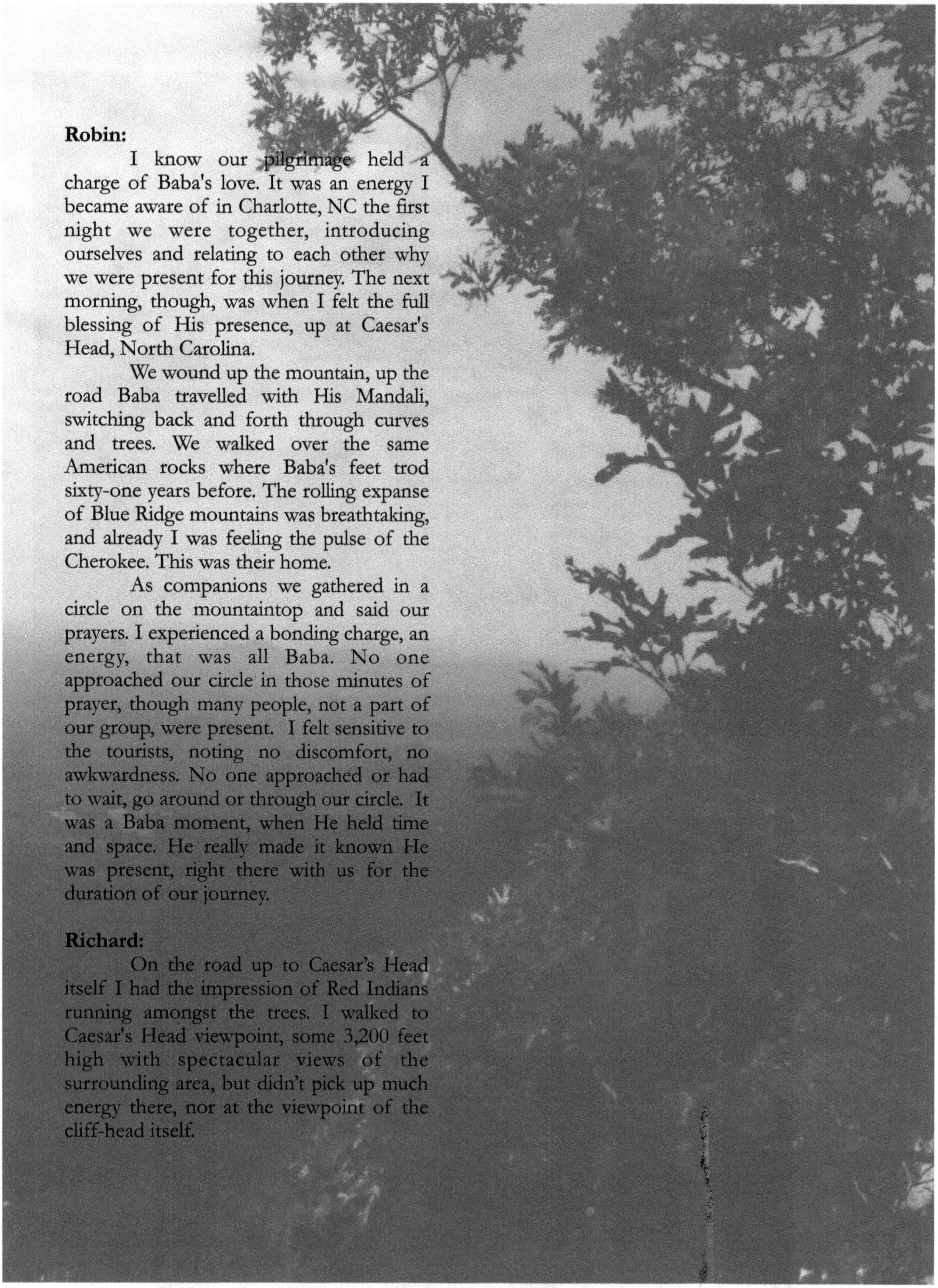

Robin:

I know our pilgrimage held a charge of Baba's love. It was an energy I became aware of in Charlotte, NC the first night we were together, introducing ourselves and relating to each other why we were present for this journey. The next morning, though, was when I felt the full blessing of His presence, up at Caesar's Head, North Carolina.

We wound up the mountain, up the road Baba travelled with His Mandali, switching back and forth through curves and trees. We walked over the same American rocks where Baba's feet trod sixty-one years before. The rolling expanse of Blue Ridge mountains was breathtaking, and already I was feeling the pulse of the Cherokee. This was their home.

As companions we gathered in a circle on the mountaintop and said our prayers. I experienced a bonding charge, an energy, that was all Baba. No one approached our circle in those minutes of prayer, though many people, not a part of our group, were present. I felt sensitive to the tourists, noting no discomfort, no awkwardness. No one approached or had to wait, go around or through our circle. It was a Baba moment, when He held time and space. He really made it known He was present, right there with us for the duration of our journey.

Richard:

On the road up to Caesar's Head itself I had the impression of Red Indians running amongst the trees. I walked to Caesar's Head viewpoint, some 3,200 feet high with spectacular views of the surrounding area, but didn't pick up much energy there, nor at the viewpoint of the cliff-head itself.

**Acknowledgment of Country —
brought by Dee Chapman from Australia**

We acknowledge the traditional custodians of the land where we are now gathered, and recognise that it continues to be sacred to them. We hail them: as the guardians of the earth and all the things that grow and breed in the soil; as trustees of the waters (the seas, the streams and rivers, the ponds and the lakes) and the rich variety of life in those waters. We thank them for passing this heritage to every people since the Dreamtime. We acknowledge the wrongs done to them by newcomers to this land and we seek to be partners with them in righting these wrongs and in living together in peace and harmony.

(This speech shows respect for the traditional custodians of a particular region or area.)

We Follow the Trail — by Irma Sheppard

We follow the Trail
hallowed by tears and blood
of those true to One Heart,
hallowed by the Creator's own Footprint.

We ride and we tread lightly,
to not erase the power and the sorrow
of their plight, but to harmonize
those efforts, those losses
with forgiveness
in order to realize God's True Intent.

With eyes of kindness for all,
we offer ourselves utterly
in Beloved God's service.

Lois:

In Cashiers, NC we met Lianna, a Cherokee woman, who led us to Silver Run Falls where we ate sack lunches. Standing knee-deep in the pool at the base of the falls, we participated as she performed the Cherokee water ceremony. She explained that while praying with open arms facing east, and open eyes focused on the sky, Cherokee reference the seven directions: north, south, east, west, the center, above and below. She said the soil was sacred and they never took soil from a place, but if we wanted to take a rock, we should first ask permission from the rock.

Lianna made each of us a beaded necklace, which included a grey corn-bead. On the Trail of Tears the Cherokee cried many tears of grief and hopelessness—one third of them died on the journey to Oklahoma. According to legend, where their tears hit the ground, a plant sprang up, whose grey seeds look like tears. In memory of that time Cherokees wear necklaces that include corn-beads.

Richard:

At Silver Run Falls we met Lianna, our First Cherokee guide, who talked about their customs over lunch, before taking us through a sacred water ceremony at the falls and at the entrance bridge on the way out. The talks were interesting. I didn't pick up on much energy by the falls, but found more by the bridge.

Anisa:

Lianna Costantino, who is from the Cherokee Coalition for Healing and Wellness, guided us to Silver Run Falls where we sang the spiritual song the Cherokee sing at morning, noon, and evening. Cherokee face east when praying and keep their eyes open during prayer to see and be seen by the Creator. We learned how to do the water ceremony. As we crossed a small bridge, we offered Cherokee tobacco to Ukten, so we could travel in his land in peace and safety. Lianna told me a bedtime story the first night, about a stick-ball game between the two-legged and the four-legged creatures. I liked it a lot.

Amazing Grace

Amazing grace! how sweet the sound,
That saved a soul like me!
I once was lost but now am found,
Was blind, but now I see.

```
         AMAZING GRACE

       U-ne-la-nv-hi U-we-tsi
       I-ga-gu-yv-he-yi
       Hna-quo-tso-sv Wi-yu-lo-se
       I-ga-gu-yv-ho-nv.

       A-se-no Yi-u-ne-tse-yi
       I-yu-no Du-le-nv
       Ta-li-ne-dv Tse-lu-tse-li
       U-dv-ne Yu-ne-tsv.
```

Robin:

Walking the trail with Lianna to Silver Run Falls, I had my first experience of how each of us was really, truly one of His 'Beads.' On the narrow path through the forest, one after another, there we were strung together as Beads-on-One-String, unique and beautiful and His. The religions as Beads and His followers coming together, in love, also as Beads.

Lois:

In Franklin we stopped at an ancient, sacred grassy mound with strong energy. We read Don Stevens' Prayer of Forgiveness, the invocation, "Acknowledgement of Country," the poem, "We Follow the Trail." We said Baba's Prayer of Repentance, and sang "Amazing Grace" in Cherokee and in English. Lianna's response was tears. She taught us the traditional rotating circle hug shared among Cherokee. Each time we spoke these prayers throughout our pilgrimage, we and our Cherokee or African-American companions were moved by their intangible power. We knew we were enveloped in Baba's Grace, more and more companions in His Love.

Richard:

At Nikwasi Mound, after hearing its history, I went for an energy search around the base, as we were not allowed on the mound itself due to its sacred nature. I discovered a broad, interesting energy line in one corner of the mound, which either came in or out of the Mound. I discussed this with Lianna and showed her the location. She told me that whenever she was on the Mound itself she experienced a tingling sensation in her hands. She also said that there were stories of warriors who appeared at crucial moments in the local history when the town was under threat. I felt the energy connected to another sacred mound of the Cherokees where they still perform ceremonies, but we needed permission to visit there.

Lois:

Beside the mound I heard the echo of Cherokee village women who seemed to be present, but hidden in the thick forests in the hills around us. I heard these women and their children doing their daily chores together from a time long before our modern intrusion. This shadowy image was present whenever we stopped in or near the woods as we moved through Cherokee lands. This presence was soothing to me.

Day 2 - September 24 — Ducktown, TN

Lois:

Our Cherokee guides, Carol and Lianna, led us to the gravesite of Nancy Ward, known as the last Beloved Woman, an 18th Century Cherokee, who maintained a bridge between the Cherokee and early American settlers. After several U-turns, Anisa, the youngest pilgrim, spotted an historical marker indicating our road to the peaceful memorial park on a hill overlooking miles of forest.

Carol and Lianna told us how the Cherokee and other American Indians suffered from being forced to give up their native languages and cultural and spiritual practices when they were sent as children to the Indian schools. Even today many older Cherokee refuse to practice the old ways because memories of their fear of retribution from Indian School staff have marked them with near PTSD reactions. We said our prayers together into the open air looking out over the rolling hills of Tennessee. It was so beautiful that Carol, Lianna and all of us were deeply touched.

Richard:

At Nancy Ward's Cemetery there was an exchange of gifts between the female tour members and Lianna and Carol. On the way to the gravesite I noticed a sign with various locations associated with the 'Trail of Tears,' which we didn't know of and missed due to time constraints. I took a photo of these locations for future reference. At the gravesite Carol talked about the Healing Coalition before we performed a ceremony. During the talk a baby dragonfly hovered around and kept landing on me till finally it rested on my fingertip until the talk finished. This was the first of several interactions with them during the trip.

Anisa:

At Nancy Ward's gravesite, we prayed for forgiveness and sang an archaic and ancient Cherokee song, which is so old that some of the words are not understood by any of the Cherokee. We put tobacco and other offerings on the gravesite.

Margaret:

Don and I are not sure we're 'Beads,' much less 'on a string,' but we're glad we participated in the Heartland Pilgrimage. We arrived in Charlotte, NC, having just driven 10,000 miles to the West Coast and back, and were happy to sit back and let someone else drive. Much as we're grateful to the four drivers, we found it hilarious that, despite GPS, MapQuest, etc., hardly a day passed without a U-turn.

Carole:

Suffice it to say that two lovely, spiritual, creative and very right-brained women planned our trip. They had only MapQuest to guide them. I began to purchase regular road maps at each stop. Of course, it was never Map Quest or my maps that guided us. It was always Baba. More U-turns were made on this trip than in any Driver Education Class. I was reminded of stories from the mandali—when Baba gave a specific set of instructions as to how to get someplace and back. Baba's faithful follower would follow the instructions—every time except once. That was exactly the time Baba needed them to be on the prescribed route. We were honored to be able to do the same thing. Repeatedly.

We were to meet with several groups of people who tend to do things 'when the time is right' rather than by the clock—Native Americans and people from the South. Soon I relaxed, knowing we'd get where we were supposed to be and see who we were supposed to see all in Baba's time. Of course, this is the only time there is.

Lois:

We had wonderful hours of conversation rolling together in the van—anecdotes from our lives and stories of Baba and the mandali. We laughed heartily over our bouts of geographic disorientation, our humorous attempts at walkie-talkie communication between vans, and the zany group antics of getting in and out of the vans for routine stops. Remembering the rules of the New Life journey helped.

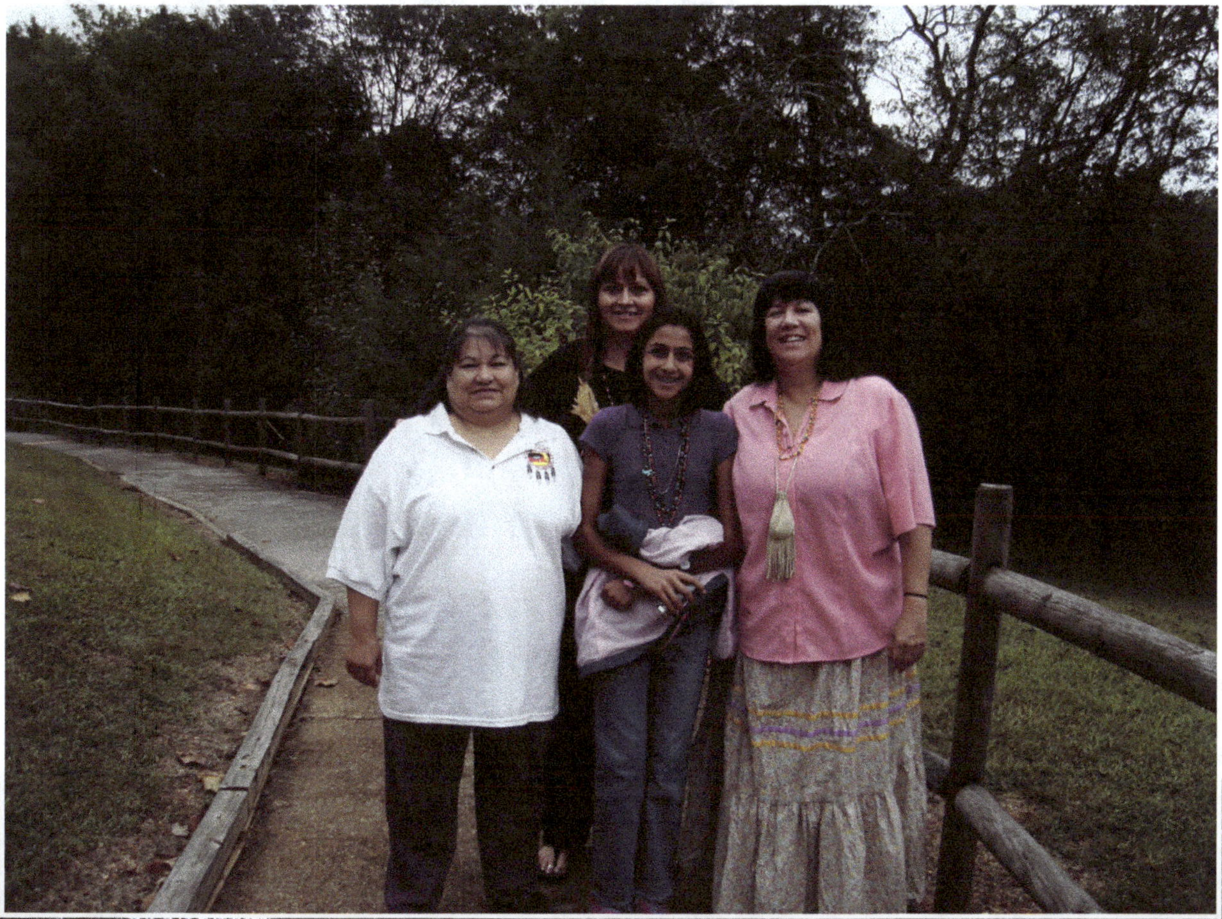

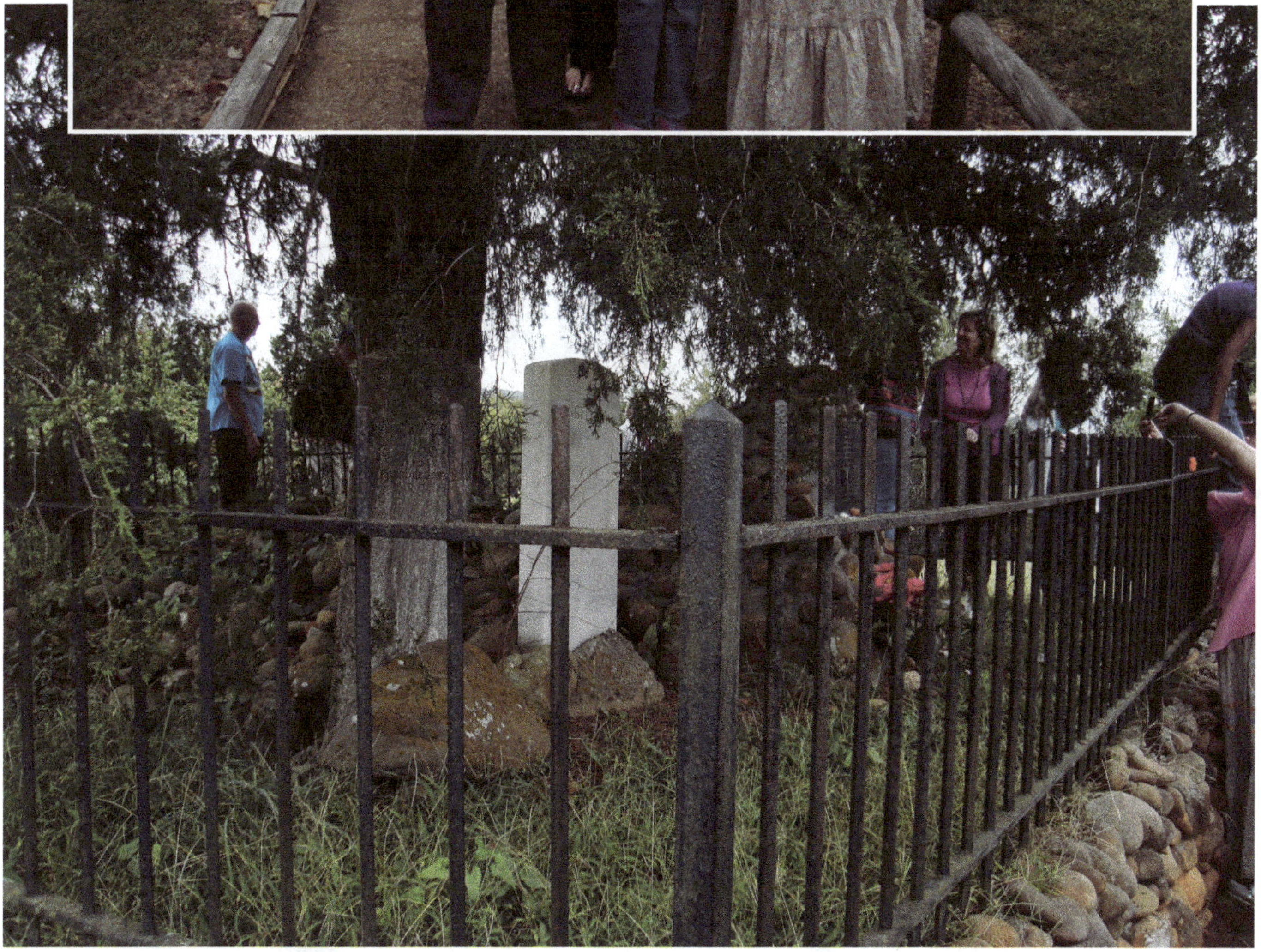

Nancy Ward's gravesite, Tennessee

Day 3- September 25 — Germantown, TN

Lois:

At Village Creek State Park in Wynne, AR some of us walked across the top of a dam and into the forest, listening to birds and watching hawks circle above. An illustrated sign told of the numbers of American Indians who had marched along The Military Road, which we approached with open but heavy hearts. Now just another path in the forest, this road had been constructed in the 1830's for the removal of thousands of members of the Cherokee, Choctaw, Seminole, Muskogee and Chickasaw nations from their traditional homelands coveted by American settlers.

Beside this "Trail of Tears" we held hands in a circle. Dee read the "Acknowledgment of Country," I read "We Follow the Trail," we chanted prayers of repentance and forgiveness and sang "Amazing Grace" in Cherokee and in English. Our voices rose into the trees and Richard's beautiful tenor voice encircled us like smoke as we asked for forgiveness from those who had passed before us through these woods. Again I saw the spirits of the Cherokee women watching us from a safe distance. They seemed to watch with passive respect as the little boys with them giggled at our modern ways. We walked back to the vans in silence, absorbing the sounds of the forest, my attention on the trees—so many steeples in God's glorious church.

Richard:

As I stepped off the road onto the grass by the lakeside path I felt a rush of energy towards and through me. It was like being greeted by a group of friends I hadn't seen for many years. This feeling stayed with me as we went alongside the lake.

We were greeted and accompanied by numerous dragonflies who treated us to wonderful aerial displays. I saw what looked like an eagle settling into its nest in the trees high above the forest.

We arrived at the Old Military Road—quite a challenge for some, together with another change in energy. Some were overcome by tears, so I decided we needed to hold hands to stabilise and focus everyone. Kathy felt the need to hang onto a tree so we arranged the circle accordingly to cross the trail. Here it felt as though we were surrounded by numerous Native Americans. The feelings grew stronger as the prayers were said, to the point that I felt the need to be playing a drum and joining in what felt like a celebration of unity and an injection of new energy for the earth.

Afterwards I felt the need to walk up the Trail some ways in both directions to clear and sense any changes. While returning from one side I met Cheryl coming from the group and she was surprised at how peaceful and untroubled it felt. I thought I could follow the trail, then loop round to meet up with the others, but couldn't find the path indicated on the map so had to retrace my footsteps. When I caught up with the others, they told me how dragonflies danced a repeated pattern in front of them for several minutes and how fascinating it was to watch them so closely and intimately before taking our leave of the State Park.

A dragonfly metamorphoses from a nymph in water to the realm of air, signifying a shift from emotion to control and balance of the mind. Their shells reflect and refract light and colour, associating them with the power of light, and the abilities of a changeling. Stories speak of them as relatives of ancient dragons, and so they are fabulous links to nature spirits and that ancient energy.

Karl:

Don, Irma and I stayed with the vans while the others trekked to the origin of the Trail of Tears. In that peaceful setting I had my first real conversation with Don. He told me the long story of the unjust accusations and legal outcomes from his work situation in the '60s. I admired and envied his equanimity then and now. "It was all Baba," he said. "It's always all Baba." I remembered his chant, "BabaBabaBaba," everyday, whatever was happening. I told Irma I'd like some of Don's attitude. She said, "Ask him. Ask him to give you some." In a moment of suspended disbelief I walked back to Don. "Don, give me some of your attitude." Chuckling, he laid his hand on top of my head, blessing me with "Avatar Meher Baba ki jai!" When Margaret returned, I told her, "Don gave me some of his attitude." "Oh no!" she said. "I mean his attitude about Baba." "Oh—that's different. That's good!"

Robin headed to the Old Military Road

Lois:

At dusk we rolled into the Cherokee Heritage Center, met by Ryan Mackey, Nathan and several women. Our Cherokee hosts seemed unfazed by our late arrival, saying we were on 'Indian time' and directed us to wooden benches in the Cherokee village. They introduced themselves and their families, saying their Cherokee names. Ryan was Wah'de. They told us about traditional Cherokee life. Women play a big role in this matrilineal culture, making decisions, but the men state them. The mother's brother trains the children as the children belong to the mother's clan.

It was dark as they led us into a ceremonial round house of packed earth construction. We walked through a seashell-curved entrance, which opened onto a dark circular room. In the center a large friendship prayer fire burned with wood placed to face the four directions. So little smoke escaped through the hole in the center of the roof that the room was alarmingly thick with smoke.

Cherokee Heritage Center, Talequah OK

Carole

I seemed to be the one that 'held the space' for tears. Many times my eyes filled, then overflowed at any and all times and places—sitting in the van watching the countryside go by, during a meal when someone related his or her personal experience, or while we were with those whom we had come to ask to forgive us.

When we were with the Cherokee, we sang Amazing Grace after the prayers, first in English, then in Cherokee. Each time we asked for forgiveness, those representing the other group said this had never happened before. They had never heard of such a thing. The Cherokee in Tahlequah, OK in turn asked our forgiveness for what their ancestors had done to us. Culturally, every time one of them was killed, someone from the family of the killer was killed. They asked our forgiveness for all of us that they had killed.

THERE'S ALWAYS A REASON — by Jill

On the Heartland pilgrimage we unwittingly contracted to take a fast ride down the rabbit hole where we became immediately disoriented. We landed squarely in Baba's labyrinth, which was distinguished by His control over the vehicle. Turning it into His toy matchbox car, He dragged it (with sheer delight I am sure) in spiraling U-turns that eventually led all participants to get much more than we bargained for. The result was not only deeply personal, but also expansive, including the selective choosing of new and completely unsuspecting beads to be strung onto His string of unity and oneness. The litmus test that proved Baba had total control of the situation was that no matter how strongly any person insisted they knew the best or correct route to our next destination, each would be wrong at some point, and sometimes in a big way. No paper map, GPS, or MapQuest search was going to override Baba's magnetic finger: U-turning us, confusing and frustrating us, delaying us for His own mysterious satisfaction.

Tahlequah is not a particularly big town. We were already late and anxious because we had some extraordinary experiences waiting for us with some very special Cherokee people. To illustrate how much control was NOT in our hands, we passed, several times, the very intersection where we were to turn to get to the Cherokee village.

Despite Walmart as a landmark, the two drivers, two navigators and eleven other people could not see where to turn. We drove seven miles beyond it, outside of town! I heard the puzzled, patient voice of Wah'de on the phone with Kathryn, sitting in the front seat next to me, trying to navigate us, communicate where we were, and translate what we needed to do. Somehow it just wouldn't happen.

First Nation people are a patient people, used to waiting. When we finally arrived, we were given a warm greeting. We had a short talking circle during which we received an explanation of the welcome dance, their gift to us. They told us the significance of the turtle shells worn on the legs of the women who kept the pace of the dance, and about the culture of the Council house, which is constructed in an octagon.

It took two U-turns to actually get inside, where the significance and sacredness of what was about to happen made its own strong presence felt. Then we discovered a new element, not experienced anywhere else, which would exponentially enhance opening to the bliss of it, at least for me—suffering.

In the center of the Council house, a huge fire pit with a few enormous cedar logs had been burning for a long time. No flames crackled on the logs, now huge coals, profusely smoking, glowing a hot yellow-orange. Earlier that day a big rainstorm left the fire pit wet. This was the atmosphere—hot dense smoke. I was sure I would need an emergency room visit after the experience. We Beads sat on benches, three deep, lining an outside wall. Wah'de, a young Cherokee chief, stood in front of the burning ember logs, talking about the dance and Cherokee tradition. He called the dance, and was joined by an older chief, his twelve-year-old son, and the women. Back and forth young and older chiefs answered each other in the Cherokee tongue. Suddenly the women began the dance with the stomp of their turtle shells. Some had as many as nine shells on each leg. The effect was powerfully accentuated as the women and men became dark silhouettes circling the amber-colored logs. Men sang and answered in the language of the dance. Women kept the rhythm with their turtle shells. The space filled with smoke and primal sounds. My attention became trance-like as I was hypnotized by these sensations. They vibrated every part of my soul. Smoke took over my senses. Spirits filled the room. In my perception, acutely clear at the time, I was transported to another dimension beyond time and space.

The dance ended, the dancers faded into the blackness and Wah'de stood before me as a silhouette and called me up to join him. No thoughts told me what to do. I got up and faced Wah'de, but he disappeared into the darkness, leaving me standing by myself. At first it was painful—difficult to breathe and speak at the same time, even while covering my nose and mouth with my scarf. I told of our troubles in getting there, our U-turns, our not being able to see what was in front of us. I said I had to trust there was a reason for it. Out of that smoky darkness the strong clear voice of Wah'de rang through the room answering, "There's always a reason."

I acknowledged the wrongs done to the Cherokee, and called to the European ancestors to be part of the spirits, to witness the apology I made on their behalf for the generational grief and suffering caused by their ignorance and greed. I spoke of our purpose. I called Irma and Dee to read their prayers in the glow of the logs. Danielle and Anisa offered more light from a cell phone. A few Beads sang along with Kathryn and Richard, a verse of Amazing Grace in Cherokee and one in English. All the Beads said the Prayer of Repentance. Our offerings caused Wah'de to reappear from the smoky darkness, to say they would offer another gift to us—the dance of friendship. We were all invited to dance together in unity with the Cherokee around those hot smoking logs—a very rare honor. Baba's Beads-On-One-String and Cherokee people danced a long dance  together that night in friendship and unity, with all defenses and pretenses erased through loving sincerity. Wah'de told me the next time we came to Tahlequah we would be welcomed to stay in the homes of the Cherokee people.

Beauty, Harmony, Love, Unity. "There's always a reason."

Margaret:
Certainly one of the most memorable experiences of the tour was dancing around the fire with the Cherokee in their smoke-filled lodge. Another was walking on the actual Trail of Tears along the lake. When we visited the grave of Nancy Ward, my respect for the D.A.R. increased immensely when I learned she was a member.

Richard:
Ryan talked about their way of life, followed by a tribal leader on his duties and the manufacture of their equipment. A lady spoke about their dances and the use of turtle shells to provide the rhythm. We saw the dancers in the Village Meeting Hut, which was rather smoky. It was difficult to see the dancers but I enjoyed the atmosphere. They asked us to join them in the dancing—difficult due to the smoke bringing tears to the eyes, but I enjoyed participating. We said the prayers and sang Amazing Grace. The Tribes people seemed impressed and asked us to join them in their more sacred dances and songs. It felt like a great honour to dance in togetherness and oneness, and there seemed to be a definite change of energy.

Irma:

Many Cherokee in Tahlequah follow traditional ways. After they related some of these to us, danced and sang around a Friendship Fire, a few accompanied us to Sam and Ella's for pizza. We sat around a long, long table. While Wah'de told more stories and answered more questions, I watched a young Cherokee mother at our end of the table.

She had three children with her: a girl about ten, a boy about seven and a girl about four. The youngest girl offered Don a trivet from the table. Being an experienced grandpa, Don took it and playfully began to 'eat' from it. Delighted, the little girl skipped off to find one trivet after another for Don, for his wife, Margaret, and others. She scoured the tables for trivets to pile on ours.

Her brother caught the excitement of this game. He grabbed a trivet to play too. But little sister reacted with: No! Mine! And they tussled. Their mother shushed them. She put her arm around her son's shoulder and said to him, *You know what Daddy always tells you—if you want the women to be happy, you have to do what they want.*

She spoke to her son in a quiet voice and the boy heard. This, a teaching from father to son, from mother to son in the matriarchal Cherokee Nation.

Day 4 - September 26 — Tahlequah, OK

Lois:

In the morning Dee sat in the dining room next to an older man who, she discovered, was the great-great-great-grandson of Cherokee Chief John Ross, who had been one of the leaders of the Cherokee tribe during the removal years. He told us Chief John Ross's grave was in Tahlequah. This fortuitous meeting was a reminder that Baba is the One who uses everything and wastes nothing, not even an early morning coffee.

For Richard Budd from Scotland, these connections with the Cherokee were of particular interest. Because of political circumstances in Scotland in the nineteenth century many Scots moved to the New World to escape persecution. Many moved into the hills and mountains of Appalachia, intermarried and had business dealings with the Cherokee who lived there. Chief John Ross's family was one of these cross-cultural matches, so meeting his great-great-great grandson was a great privilege.

In Prague we picked up carnations at the florist and drove to Baba's accident site. The body of a raccoon lay in front of the site and a dead rattlesnake a few feet away. We laid carnations on the site, sat quietly, then said the Parvardigar Prayer, the Prayer of Repentance and the Beloved God Prayer.

This was my first visit to the accident site since I came to Baba in 1974. Seeing this spot was very significant to me. I remembered how in May, 1970, as a newlywed and a Vista volunteer stationed in Oklahoma, I'd become overwhelmed with tears, as I watched a pantomimed play set to music from The Who's opera "Tommy," at a theater just ten to fifteen miles from Baba's accident site.

The Heartland Center staff was very welcoming, showing the first timers around the Burleson House with its lovely photos of Baba. I was taken to the hospital next door. Both the room where Baba stayed after the accident and Mehera, Mehru and Mani's room were currently used for other purposes, yet I could see and feel where Baba had lain without being told. I felt him smiling at my arrival and gesturing to me to 'come closer, come closer.' Many thanks to the Heartland Center staff for a wonderful lunch of lentils and rice, beet salad, raita, and oatmeal cookies.

Meher Baba's accident site outside Prague, Oklahoma

Carole:

Many of the pilgrims had never visited the Heartland Center in Prague. Being originally from Oklahoma, I have visited several times and dearly loved each experience. I hoped my fellow pilgrims would feel Baba's presence in the entire town of Prague, as I do, and fall in love with it as I have. After all those miles and hours in the vans, all those early mornings and late nights, we spent only three hours in Prague. In spite of the short span of time there, Baba made sure this was one of the most magical times of the Pilgrimage and also one of the best visits I have had at the Heartland Center.

Richard:

At the florist shop we collected flowers. Carole believed the laundry opposite was where the women Mandali went while attending Baba and the others. Later we were told that the present florist shop was where the laundry had been in Baba's time.

Philip White took us to the accident spot. I felt excited as we drew near the spot and noticed a raccoon was knocked down at the spot where Baba's accident occurred. Everyone gathered round and laid flowers on the accident spot. I was surprised the energy there was not that strong. As I sat on the grass verge, grasshoppers landed on my legs. Anisa laid flowers connecting the raccoon to Baba's accident spot.

At midday Dan Sparks took a group of us to tour the hospital. Initially I had to clear access to the rooms where Baba and Mehera were treated. First we went to the room where Baba was treated. After inspecting the room, I found the spot where Baba's bed had been located next to the window, opposite the entrance from the corridor. Carole, Kathy and some others followed my lead when I told them of the location of the spot. I asked Dan if he knew where Baba's bed had been located. He said he didn't know, so I told him where it had been located in the room. Next we went to Mehera's and Elizabeth's room. Even before entering the room I felt a beautiful energy there, which was so loving and enveloping. I searched and located

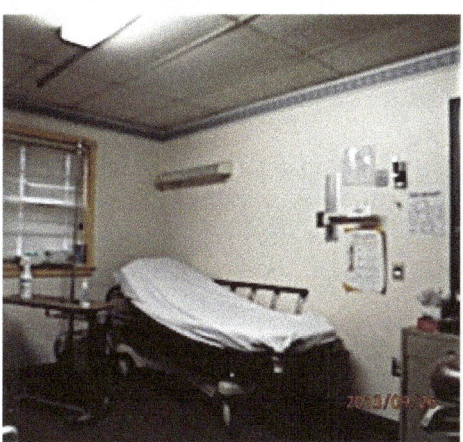
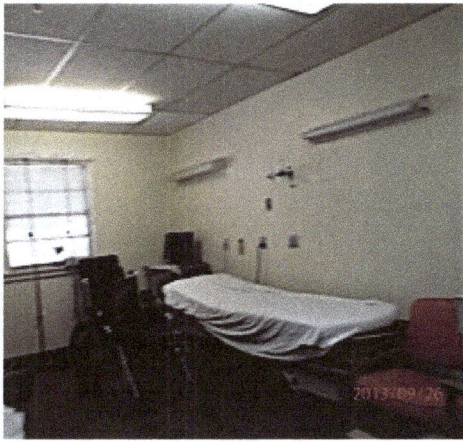

the position of Mehera's bed and then where Elizabeth's had been situated.

Initially I felt this was the end of the connection with the Native American energy, but was delighted to be proved wrong.

Ginna Bourisseau, Managing Director, Avatar Meher Baba Heartland Center:

Inspired by the tours in Europe led by Don Stevens, a group of travelers in search of where Baba touched this continent left Charlotte, NC, in two vans ....With much anticipation local Baba lovers and I welcomed them to the Heartland Center on September 26, after they had spent the night in Tahlequah, OK, capital of the Cherokee Nation.

They arrived in Prague around ten a.m.. They needed to leave by twelve-thirty p.m., so it was a challenge to handle fifteen people, shepherding them to the accident site, the Prague hospital to see Baba's room, bathrooms, and lunch. Local Baba lovers, Dan Sparks and Phillip White, pitched in to make the event go smoothly. Phillip took everyone to the accident site. The group spread flowers over the ground at the accident site. Prayers were offered to dear Baba.

When they returned from the accident site we did some quick tours of the house and gave a history of Dr. Burleson and his family. Carole Cunningham led one of the groups through the house. Dan took shifts of people over to the hospital and others stayed to eat lunch. Then the groups shifted places. Lynn Wilhite arrived and held court in the Library. Lunch was followed by plenty of chai and cookies, enough that they packed little bags of cookies and grapes for the road.

The time spent drinking the wine of the Avatar was short and bittersweet—barely enough time to understand and feel what a special place the Heartland Center is. For some it was a very long journey—from Australia and from Scotland. It was a joyous and Baba-filled time.

Lois:

We had at least a seven-hour drive back across Oklahoma and Arkansas to reach Clarksdale, MS. There we met Catherine Burks-Brooks, one of the Freedom Riders, at the Ground Zero Blues Club that night. On the surface of every column, wall and table in the Club people had written messages. Razor Blades, an elderly black man, a local favorite, dressed in slick trousers and a fedora joined the professionals for a few songs. His voice rang out with smooth, buttery Blues tunes that belied his years. As we left, we saw our lovely, twenty-year-old Kiva visiting outside with several local white boys, whose accents were pure Mississippi country boy. When we told them why we were in Clarksdale, and that one of the actual Freedom Riders was with us, they stood to meet her with appropriate respect when she came out.

Anisa:

We met a Freedom Rider, Catherine, at the Ground Zero Blues Club on jam night. On the way we passed the Crossroads, where the blues started. People from all over the world played harmonica they'd learned in a class recently. It was awesome.

Karl:

In the van the day after visiting the Ground Zero Blues Club, I mentioned to Catherine how it seemed that most fans and many performers of the modern Blues scene were white. She sighed and said Blues music was "embarrassing to Blacks of all ages." She said the old Delta Blues reminded them of post-slavery sharecropping. The upbeat Chicago Rhythm and Blues that came later, the precursor to '50s Rock 'n' Roll, reminded them of the Jim Crow '40s and '50s—prejudice only recently left behind. Catherine smiled and said, "Since the early 1960's, just as the Civil Rights movement got underway, the Blues has belonged to white people."

Catherine Burks-Brooks © Associated Press

Ground Zero Blues Club, Clarksdale, MS.

Karl:

The photo to the right is a historical spot, the legendary crossroads in Clarksdale where bluesman Robert Johnson supposedly sold his soul to the Devil in exchange for blues immortality. His song 'Crossroads' was one of the finest cover songs by Eric Clapton and Cream. This site is also the inspiration for Bob Dylan's song and album 'Highway 61 Revisited'.

Day 5 - September 27 — Clarksdale, MS

Lois:

We breakfasted with Catherine Burks-Brooks at the Yazoo Pass coffee shop. Catherine was an elegant African-American in her mid-seventies, with first-hand stories of her years as a civil rights activist in Mississippi and Alabama in the 1960s. People kept coming up to us asking, "Where y'all from and why are y'all in Clarksdayull?" One fellow told us the restaurant we were in had once been the local Woolworths store, where some Freedom Riders had sat at the counter.

At Parchman State Penitentiary I expected we'd be run through the same searches and background checks routine for visitors to Oregon State Penitentiary where I'd been a teacher for 20 years. But the Mississippi Department of Corrections welcomed us warmly, only asking us to leave behind cell phones and cameras before entering the prison grounds. Parchman was situated on twenty-eight square miles of Delta farmland. Most inmates worked the cotton crops. It housed the state's male death row inmates. Historically inmates who passed years of their lives in Parchman Farm sang about their miseries, so this prison is actually the birthplace of the 'Blues.'

In the spring of 1961 civil rights protesters called Freedom Riders were riding Greyhound buses across the South to challenge the unconstitutional segregation of the public facilities serving interstate transportation. Freedom Riders were arrested when they reached Jackson, MS, and sentenced to Parchman Prison. Food was poor and limited. Catherine remembered they sang freedom songs non-stop in their cell-block to raise spirits and build unity. Prison authorities removed their

Parchman State Penitentiary

mattresses and the bug screens from the windows, so the thick hum of the Delta's mosquitoes filled their cells. Catherine shared that she has since had a near phobia of insects.

Officers escorted us to Cell Block 17. First we passed a chamber with a primitive electric chair. In the next cell was the table for current executions. A row of cells followed, empty of inmates now, where Catherine and others had been held in 1961. I'd often walked in the cellblocks of Oregon State Penitentiary, but this block of empty cells emanated the pain, loss and anger of the 304 Freedom Riders imprisoned there in 1961.

Catherine related memories of her time imprisoned here. We joined hands, expressed our invocation to Catherine as a representative of the history of the viciousness of racism these cells expressed so loudly. We read "We Follow the Trail," said the Prayer of Repentance, and stood in Baba's silence for a moment. As we left the building, the tall Black captain who led us into the block and listened as we asked for forgiveness for our country's history of prejudice, called Jill back. He took her hands in his and said, *"I don't know what ya'll are doing, but that was a real good thing you did in there, a real good thing. Thank you."*

Margaret:

In Clarksdale, MS Don and I skipped the visit to Parchman State Prison rather than get special permission from the Warden. In the meantime Don got a huge charge out of chatting up the good old boys at the Yazoo Pass diner who were so curious as to what our group was doing in their town. The town fathers assured Don that things were getting better in Clarksdale.

Roberts' Sunday Dinner,
Birmingham, Alabama

Lois:

In Birmingham, AL we went to Roberts' Sunday Dinner, a small neighborhood eatery for a private catered dinner Jill had arranged for us. We settled ourselves at the few tables and Mr. and Mrs. Roberts, the black couple who owned the place, along with one helper, began to serve our meal. We started with iced tea and appetizers of hot grits with Cajun sausage, hot peppers and shrimp. Then we filed past a row of warmers filled with savory tender roasted pork, fried chicken wings, ribs with barbeque sauce, very tender boiled collard greens (the best we had the whole trip), fresh green beans cooked with bacon and new potatoes, crazy sweet yams cooked with butterscotch, creamy macaroni dripping with cheese, crispy Southern cornbread, freshly baked rolls and butter, and peach cobbler for dessert. There was a lot of food, but honestly, every bite was so delicious I just couldn't stop eating. We'd really been treated to a great example of Southern black cuisine. I felt privileged to be a guest at the Roberts' eatery.

Day 6 - September 28 — Birmingham, AL

Lois:

At 9:50 a.m. we pulled up to the 16th St. Baptist Church. Mr. Washington, the church administrator, said a group was expected for a 10:00 tour, but we could look at the museum on the lower level. At 10:15 Mr. Washington said the group called from New Orleans to say they were late, so we could take their place in the front pews of the sanctuary. As part of his tour lecture we watched a video on the role the church played during the Civil Rights era, and the history of the 1963 bombing which killed four young girls.

A large stained glass window was left intact except for the face of Jesus, which was blown out. A Danish artist donated a stained glass window to be placed behind the balcony, depicting Jesus with arms extended, his right hand pushing against oppression, his left hand open, reaching toward reconciliation and harmony. Jesus's quote, *"As you do to the least of them, you do it to me,"* is written across this exquisite piece of glass art.

An African-American youth group arrived early from the Chattanooga Baptist Church. At Mr. Washington's invitation, Jill explained we were following the Trail of Tears and the route of the Freedom Riders on a pilgrimage of forgiveness for the history of America's ill treatment of Native Americans and African-Americans.

When the video was finished, permission was granted for us to say our prayers. We stood facing the youth group and said Baba's Prayer of Repentance. Many of them came forward to greet us individually, to share hugs and comments on the power of the Prayer of Repentance. Baba's prayer said what we held in our hearts and more, and something important had been heard. After Mr. Washington led the youth group to the museum downstairs, Karl went to the grand piano that sat before us. Slowly the notes of the Gujarati Arti filled the sanctuary with its healing power.

Richard:

I walked down the aisle but didn't feel any particular energy, even when stopping to pray at the altar. Jill was confronted by a member, who said we were not allowed in the church. She explained we had permission. We went down to the archives room to take in the history of the Civil Rights events from 1957 to the bombing of the church, to final agreement by the City Council to stop segregation in the mid- 60's.

One of the members said their ten a.m. tour had cancelled and we could replace them. Baba, what a blessing! It was obvious to me He was at work—as I climbed the stairs back to the church I felt the energy building. By the time I stepped into the church there was this wonderful energy of love.

Carole:

The most emotional stop for me was the 16th Street Baptist Church, the site of the bombing that killed four Negro girls in the sixties. Entering the sanctuary, we were greeted by the altar and a bright red carpet. I immediately

Kathryn:

This sculpture, dedicated to the Four Girls, is called "The Love That Forgives." The title is based on the Sunday school lesson the girls were studying at the time they died. It was on the Biblical chapter where Joseph forgives his brothers for having sold him into slavery.

burst into sobs, sat down in the nearest pew and cried uncontrollably. I seemed to experience the same pain and suffering that had occurred there. It seemed to hang in the air over all.

Downstairs were displays and mementoes of the bombing. Representative items from the four girls who were killed hung on the wall—school pictures and their little dresses flattened and framed. One spelled her name, Carole, with an 'e' just as I do.

I couldn't stay long in the church—the sorrow and pain were too much for me. In a near panic, I asked a guard for the quickest way out and almost ran in the direction of the exit. Warm, bright sunlight greeted me as I walked out and breathed a sigh of relief. Outside I relaxed with other pilgrims and we talked about our experiences.

These historical events occurred while I was growing up, but I was unaware of their gravity. From the outset, I hadn't wanted to do this part of the pilgrimage. I know now this part of my life made much more of an impression on me than I realized.

Irma:

As we recited the Prayer of Repentance, I made eye contact with the young people as we said each phrase. Our prayers ended, Jill stepped toward the leader of the youth group and they embraced. Many of us embraced each other. At the end, two small boys, about four, stood backed up against their father's legs. Eyes wide, they looked up at me. The father and I exchanged smiles. He gently nudged his boys forward. I knelt and hugged them. We parted with smiles.

Downstairs in the church, we examined photographs, testimonials and plaques commemorating the African-Americans' trials, faith and fortitude in gaining acknowledgment of their rights to human dignity. Someone from the church came to one of our group asking for a copy of the Prayer of Repentance.

Anisa:
We prayed facing the church group. They cried and blessed us a lot. We crossed the street to the Civil Rights Institution, watched a video on segregation, how Blacks were the foundation of Birmingham, building its railroads, mines, and buildings. A wall opened to a large exhibit on early Birmingham, featuring the early segregated schools in Birmingham and separate water fountains for whites and Blacks.

Forgiveness —
by Anisa Shah (with some help from her mom, Danielle Shah, who is not a writer)

Forgiveness is like a butterfly's kiss,
a soft brush,
but a big impact.
Through many dark ages we have entered,
but came through into the light.
Through acts of hate,
prejudice,
and greed,
a nation has been terrorized.
But forgiveness will break through
this greatest darkness.
Through acts of prayer,
repentance,
and empathy,
verbalizing that we understand
what we have done wrong
and making apologies known.
Asking for forgiveness,
whether it be taken or not,
we've tried
to repent for our misdeeds
done to the people of this land
and many others.
Apologetic vibrations flow
throughout the universe;
healing energies
connect hearts
otherwise unknown;
feelings intertwine
creating something beautiful.

"City Within a City" mural, West Anniston, Alabama

Lois:

Our first stop in Anniston, AL was the bus station to meet Miz Georgia Calhoun, a dignified black woman and retired teacher. A life-size replica of the Greyhound bus was painted on a brick wall, with factual information about events of that day printed on signs posted around the painting. Miz Calhoun told us an angry crowd had met the bus at the Greyhound station that day in 1961 and slashed its tires. The bus had to stop outside of town where it was attacked by white crowds and set afire.

We related the mission of our pilgrimage and stood together in a circle to say our prayers of forgiveness and repentance. Miz Calhoun embraced each of us warmly, said she had never heard a more complete prayer and asked for a copy of it. Baba's prayer repeatedly brought our connections with others to the heart level, deeply moving whoever heard it. Our job was to say the prayer—Baba did the rest.

In West Anniston we saw a mural entitled "A City within a City," representing how lively it had once been: kids skating, a big church, Buffalo soldiers housed in the neighborhood during WWII, the pipe factory where nearly everybody worked.

At a diner across the street we ordered lunches. The kitchen crew scrambled to cook so many orders all at once. Some locals were there, being sociable or watching football on TV. People began asking us questions, wondering what these white folks were doing in their neighborhood where whites from East Anniston rarely ventured. They said this little eatery in the black part of town never had a white patron before. One well-dressed, but nearly toothless older woman was so impressed we'd come that she kept repeating, *"I'll never forget this; no siree, I'll never forget this."*

Margaret

In the segregated section of Anniston, we entered a local diner. An imposing black man in a tuxedo stood motionless at the entrance. On the way out, I asked if he was the owner. He said no, his wife worked there—he was dressed for a funeral. I said, "Well, you look mighty pretty," and his forbidding countenance broke into a big smile. It turned out his rapt attention was focused on the TV ball game overhead.

Lois:

General Jackson, a humble man in his mid-sixties, seemed surprised to see us in his little diner. We followed him and Barbara Boyd, the State Representative, to the actual

General Jackson and Lois talk in front of his restaurant

site of the 1961 burning of the Freedom Riders' bus, where a memorial park was being proposed. They told us how white neighbors had taken in wounded Freedom Riders during the rock throwing and fire. We said Baba's Prayer of Repentance here where so much anger and pain had been released. General Jackson kept shaking his head, commenting on what a fine prayer it was, *"My, that prayer is really something, my oh my, really something."*

Anisa:

In Anniston we met Georgia Calhoun and Peter Conroy and learned about the burning and attacked buses. We prayed for forgiveness. Georgia hugged us in the Cherokee style, which we had just learned from Lianna. We hugged in a snake-like string, going around a circle of people and having every person being hugged by everybody. We went to West Anniston, west of the train tracks where the population is about 98% black. They were surprised to see thirteen white people. A mural showed West Anniston as "A City within a City," self-sustaining, little need to cross the tracks. We had lunch at General Jackson's diner. General is his actual first name. Some of us also saw his shoe shine shop next door, with photos and paintings of Martin Luther King and the burning bus.

We had dinner at Classic on Noble—extremely fancy. General Jackson told us about his life, how the blacks suffered. He nicknamed me "Little Bit." He said we made his day, having cried during the prayer for forgiveness. I told him he'd made my life. This was an amazing, uplifting experience I will never forget. I liked making a difference in people's lives and touching their hearts in ways I had never dreamt of before. I learned so much about how to live a true life, about all that has happened in the past and all that a simple sorry can do.

Pilgrimage
by Anisa Shah (with a bit of help from her mother, Danielle Shah)

Through hills and valleys we travel,
through these same ups and downs
we change—
our perspectives,
our opinions,
our understanding
of the world,
ourselves
and these hills and valleys we live in.
Its true history,
its true potential,
discovered, unlocked,
and unleashed through a journey.
Though turmoil may come on this journey,
the outcome of it is life-changing.
It's amazing how so much
can come out of one journey,
how so much change can occur
through one journey,
through one pilgrimage,
is beyond any expectations.

Day 7 - September 29 — Atlanta, GA

Lois:

We had a six-hour drive to Myrtle Beach, SC, Baba's Home in the West. Meher Spiritual Center is one of the most beautiful places on earth—virgin woods, swampy marshes, lakes, beaches, and simple cabins to cradle visitors. The tranquility soothes and the persistent care given to the Center's grounds and buildings delights the soul. All this because it is the home of the Beloved, who graced many of the Center's buildings and paths with His physical presence and love. Usually I sleep long and deeply at the Meher Center. I rarely even talk while I'm there, which is very unlike me. The Center is truly a place to enjoy a spiritual retreat in its purest form.

Enchantment of the Great Blue Heron —by Jill

Finally, the straight road home. Surely there could be no U-turns now, no mishaps, no communication gaps. We were done, did what we came to do, and more. Few cars were on the gorgeous, peaceful road to Baba's sanctuary, giving me a much-needed opportunity to concentrate on getting to Myrtle Beach. In a most appreciative state of mind, I was glad not even a billboard disturbed this expanse.

Gazing casually into that expanse, directly in front of us, I noticed a disturbance that fixed my attention—a spot of grey vibration. Growing quickly, it became a large wingspan, a distinctive shape. Oh. My. God. It was a Great Blue Heron, heading right into me, in the middle of my lane. Oh please Baba, don't let me hit it head on!!! I became so transfixed by the image so magically, yet deliberately, aiming itself at the van that my mind went blank. Apparently having no way out I just watched, but I wasn't scared.

The heron swooped above and to one side of our van. Close call. Again, it swooped up and around, around and up, circling us, dancing with us, *staying* with us as we went at least 55 mph. So agile! It even flew right next to me on the driver's side, close enough that I got a super charge and a great look at the grace, size and beauty of it. I felt so calm. Like it was mystically planned. Our highway heron performed an elaborate pattern around the van as we sped down the highway. Unknown mission accomplished, it swooped off to the van behind us. I watched as it gave them a couple of passes too. Then up into the sky and—poof, it was gone.

In Africa, the Heron was thought to communicate with the Gods.

According to North American Native tradition, the Blue Heron brings messages of self-determination and self-reliance. They represent an ability to progress and evolve, having the innate wisdom of being able to maneuver through life and co-create their own circumstances. Blue Herons reflect a need for those with this totem to follow their own unique wisdom and path of self-determination. These individuals know what is best for themselves and need to follow their hearts.

This is the message that Blue Heron brings.

Cheryl:
The place where we saw the Great Blue Heron was on Route 22, coming directly East towards Meher Spiritual Center.

Lois:

Our stay at the Center was a short three nights, but I had many hours of quiet time in the Guesthouse, wandered the trails, visited Baba's house, drank tea with others in the Original Kitchen, took long Center naps, and shared a potluck meal and feedback meeting with my pilgrimage companions. I had a wonderful stay at the Center, a perfect stay, in fact. It was long enough for Baba to fill my heart as if it had been a much longer retreat. The stops at the Heartland Center and the Meher Retreat Center had worked as bookends to the volumes we'd experienced between.

Adele Wolkin

A Moment — Irma

I first met Adele Wolkin on June 13, 1980 at the Avatar Meher Baba Center of Southern California in Los Angeles. Weeks before, I'd been graced, according to Don Stevens, by the Presence of the Master. At my first Baba meeting, Adele sat two rows ahead of me. She turned to ask me a question, just as if I would know the answer. With big, clear blue eyes she looked at me as if she'd known me all my life.

At the end of September 2013, I met Adele at the Meher Spiritual Center in Myrtle Beach, where she now resided. I was one of fifteen Baba lovers who participated in the Heartland Beads-on-One-String Pilgrimage, which concluded at the Center. I was looking forward to seeing Adele and Judy Mangold, her companion, since I hadn't seen them in a few years. Adele, ninety-five now, walked slowly as we made our way into the Original Kitchen. She wanted to hear about our journey.

After we passed through the kitchen and dining room, we had to take two steps up into the lounge. Standing behind Adele, I saw our Beads-on-One-String group coordinator, Jill English, standing on the top step. Adele asked her name and looked closely into Jill's eyes. When Jill said her name, Adele immediately cradled Jill's cheeks gently in her two hands, still looking intently into her eyes.

Adele caressed Jill's face, and said, "Oh my dear, you look just like a child of Baba's. You look like you belong in Elizabeth's [Patterson] group..." Adele was interrupted and unable to finish her thought. I said to Jill, "This is something to write about." Jill later said this moment came as a huge Baba validation gift to her.

In the lounge I sat next to Adele as she chatted with the Heartland Beads. She held my hand, and spoke to me, once again, as if she'd known me all my life.

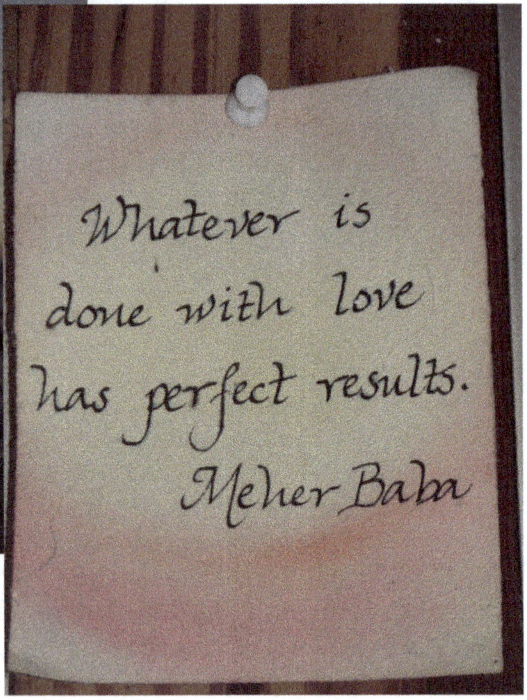

Richard:

We arrived at Myrtle Beach in the dark, happy to know we would be stationary for several days, able to rest up and savour Baba's wonderful energy in His Home in the West. I visited Yaupon Dunes, which should be part of the Trail of Tears Pilgrimage, as that is where Baba, Mehera, Elizabeth and Meheru recovered on returning to Myrtle Beach. The energy was amazing in front of the building. I located an energy spot near its rear entrance.

Upon our arrival at Myrtle Beach I realized we were reconnecting with Native American energy, as Myrtle Beach was effectively Native American territory and still retains some of that energy. I believe it is no small coincidence that Baba chose this area as His home in the West.

AFTER

Jill:

There is now a pilgrimage after the pilgrimage to be experienced, as we sort out the impact of the 'impressions' we received in action. So many powerful images flood my mind, I feel suspended in an altered state of awareness—it feels so real. These experiences can be life changing, especially as we reflect on their meaning to us. Many moments are coming to awareness now that I wasn't able to focus on at the time of their happening, and  which I simply observed at the time. Certain looks exchanged between companions, snippets of conversations I heard in passing at gas stops, bathroom lines, picnics, restaurants, the gatherings for prayers. All these wove the fabric of our network in the field, our offerings of love to the Avatar Himself. Blessings to all companions in your pilgrimage after the pilgrimage.

Our pilgrimage route is a real parallel: He traversed the route of the Trail of Tears on His way to His accident; then traversed parts of the Freedom Rider routes, Himself broken, on His way back from His accident in the ambulance to Myrtle Beach, going through many places where descendants of slaves suffered torture and death.

It wasn't *us* making all those U-turns after all! Baba surely drove us inside a labyrinth constructed just for us! I am mostly enjoying this disorientation. It feels dreamy—more in harmony with all that could be pressing stress in the way of chores. I find they are patient. Hello dust, hi there dishes, a morning nod to you leaves all over the yard, oh my dear vacuum, I've tripped over you again...

Robin:

In the days after my dream, as I reflected on its meaning, I felt that my task was to insert a conduit—somehow I was a conduit to the conduit, and Baba was using us to create an opening so He could transmit through it whatever He needed to send.

On the Pilgrimage I absolutely felt that was happening everywhere we went—He was the driver getting us to the places He wanted us. We were unwitting sheaths and conduits—Baba was flowing through us. What that means, I do not pretend to know. This was His. I didn't know Don Stevens or much about the Beads before the trip. I had little clue why I was on the trip, but had no doubt Baba wanted me there.

A few weeks ago I went to our acupuncturist, Dr. Silva, referenced in my dream. She knew little about our journey but I told her about my task in the dream and asked for her 'take' on where I was inserting the 'sheath.' She said, "Show me on my back." I put my fingers exactly where I remember from the dream. She said with a beautiful smile, *"You were there to open hearts. That is where we place a needle to open the heart center."*

Lois:

Home from the pilgrimage for nearly a month, I still find it difficult to explain to curious friends and family the ways this pilgrimage was a grand adventure, a fascinating educational experience, and an awakening of a deep sense of compassion and empathy. More importantly, and more difficult to explain, is that the pilgrimage was an experience that seems to have shifted something deep within all of us companions on the journey. This shifting is unsettling yet invaluable for most of us, but with time we will discover how its subtle power will play out in our lives.

The Heartland Pilgrimage was not about the places we visited, though historically and culturally fascinating, often in settings so beautiful my chest swelled with awe. Nor was it about the interest we felt for the people we met along our way and the fascinating stories they shared with us, though their faces and tales are filed in my heart's deep memory. Telling the story of the pilgrimage is not about the who, the what, the where or the how of the journey, though those things are absorbing and often humorous—but something else, something each day we marveled at, cocked our heads at the mystery of, held hands silently sharing with each other. The real story is that something changed us from fifteen strangers traveling in two vans into spiritual companions sharing in the great, intoxicating abstraction of sharing love with others. We experienced personal and spiritual humility and witnessed its impact on ourselves and others, including random bystanders and new acquaintances.

Letter from Lianna:

"... (Our) visit has been one of hope, cooperation and genuine friendship that I believe will grow and last...blazed a trail here where others have failed. We greatly look forward to expanding this relationship in the future in a good way as well. Your people are quite welcome here, thanks to Jill. With all the trauma our people have suffered, and the forced conversion and boarding schools we endured, proselytization is not something we appreciate....we would love to continue working with her and you all in the future."

Blessings upon you all,
With love, Lianna

Letter from Mary Herr:

Hello Jill!

On behalf of the Healing and Wellness Coalition in Cherokee, I want to thank you and Beads-on-One-String for your $300 donation, the beautiful tablecloth and the book about Native American women. Please share this with others in your group who were so generous. Your generosity is greatly appreciated.

Carol Long and Lianna Costantino enjoyed meeting you and your group and were impressed with the international aspect of Beads-on-One-String. We discussed the possibility of a stop in Cherokee at Kituwah Mound for a future pilgrimage.

Best wishes to you and Beads on One String as you plan future events.
Sincerely,
Mary A. Herr, Treasurer, Healing and Wellness Coalition

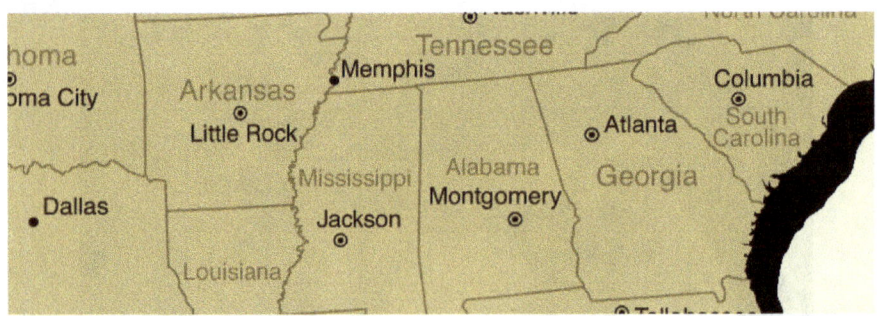

Carole:

These questions were asked of me by friends and family upon my return: "How was your trip?" "How was your vacation?" I hesitated to answer them. Firstly, it wasn't a trip—it was a trek. Secondly, it was not a vacation—it was a pilgrimage.

Each participant had different wants and expectations of the pilgrimage. I don't know how it was for everyone else, but very few of my expectations were met. At the same time it was the most perfect trip I could imagine taking in these circumstances. Baba's hand was in every turn of the road and in every event that took place.

Dhiresha:

I always felt Heartland to be a meditation on forgiveness, starting with myself and my own life. I am uncomfortable with the concept of 'doing' anything, other than joining with other lovers of God/Spirit/Life, together focusing on our few prayers, attending to the inner work, and letting Baba do the rest.

I do not see myself as giving anything, contributing to healing, helping anyone, spreading Baba's love or anything like that. I feel that pilgrimage is very personal and about our own process, our own coming home.

That is not to say that people do not get illuminated, healed or helped by the work on the pilgrimage, but from where I sit, it is not our business. It is too easy to taint that aspect with our own projections, desires, unfulfilled needs, and in this way the energy created may become muddied, lessened, familiarised or owned somehow.

I feel from my own experience of two pilgrimages, and sharing with others, that more than anything else, Beads-On-One-String pilgrimages are an introduction to and training in The New Life—skills essential for living now at this moment in time.

What This Pilgrimage Meant To Me
 — **by Anisa Shah**

This pilgrimage
opened my eyes to the world around me.
It showed me what
had been so plain in sight
but missed by my eyes,
which were playing tricks on me.
"Everything's all right"
"Everything's just fine."
Maybe in MY small world,
but not everywhere.
Just look around at all the world—
the turmoil
and the hurt.
The wars and battles being fought outside,
but there's one being fought inside our home,
the one which gets no attention,
while help goes out to other countries.
Have they forgotten about us?
Well, what I've learned on this journey
is that all of the above is true.
I've learned that forgiveness can
make a difference in people's lives,
that after hundreds of years of mistreatment
a group full of apologies
can change everything—
the bitterness,
the hatred,
the stereotypes—
all dissolve into thin air.
This pilgrimage has taught me how
to truly say sorry from the heart,
to sympathize with others' pain
and to empathize as well.
To see the light side of every situation,
and the underlying dark side as well.
This pilgrimage has taught me
that I can believe in things
and not worry what other people think,
not worry about going against others' beliefs.

Kathryn:

We keep looking for our companions, but they can only be found inside us. We are still very much marinating in the enormous personal impact of this experience.

Robin:

This was a pilgrimage of Connection and Oneness.

Lois:

The pilgrimage does indeed go on. We said prayers of forgiveness together, but I think we projected our personal feelings of humility and the powerful presence of Baba's love. Weren't we lucky!

Carole:

What we did was straight from the heart—only love and forgiveness intended. From my observation that is what was received, mirrored and given back to us. Wherever we went, we left behind a beginning of healing for all people touched by past events.

Kathryn:

Engaged together in our humble ceremony, with its various elements, we deeply entrained to each other and to our shared purpose. We then witnessed previously static conditions shifting into a dynamic state of change. We became a pivot for turning outmoded, calcified thought forms upside down.

We all suffer from outmoded thought forms. Any conscious person living in America suffers some form of collective trauma from the hypocrisy in our history, when our stated values, 'doctrines' of human dignity and freedom of religion were treated as nonexistent. It's the unbearable elephant in the living room.

There was no knowing, on our part, of what might happen on this trip. The Master of Timing had it all in His blueprint, no doubt, but we mere mortals watched in amazement as the building went up, the old one razed, before our very eyes.

Since coming back I find myself exhausted—sleeping and sleeping, and in between I go to work. I've come down with something unlike anything I've ever experienced—a roaring in my ears, affecting my hearing. I can barely hear myself speak through this muffled roar. It has made it such that silence is easier than speaking.

Richard:

I believe we are thinking too small of ourselves, i.e. just this physical body, when as Baba would say, "I am not this physical body, this is an illusion."

We are wonderful bundles of energy, constantly revolving in a kaleidoscope of colour. Each of us has a unique set of colours according to our experiences, not just in this life but also from the past—a vortex of ever-changing colour and shape according to how we interact with our surroundings, which are not solid objects either, but purely simplified by the mind for ease of understanding.

On 22nd September, along came fifteen individual vortices with a common intent and what happened? They blended together like any form of energy to form a larger energy mix. Imagine a series of small tornadoes coming together—forming a very large impress force. This is what we became as we journeyed along, like the white tornado in the adverts, cleansing everything in its path.

In coming together in the accumulative energy, we raised our own individual energies to the level of the common blend, as energy can neither be created nor destroyed, only changed in some manner. When we separated from that common energy level, we then re-settled, not to our old level, but to a higher vibrational level than before.

It is, therefore, not surprising that we have difficulty settling into our old routine, as it is like trying to put a square peg in a round hole. We are operating at a different level to what we were previously, and it manifests in many ways—changes in likes and dislikes of food, clothes, colours, music, even friends.

Irma:

Richard has described in abundant richness my thought that something shifted within us on this pilgrimage, and that we are adjusting to that shift on all levels, and that takes time. Lots of it. One thing I am aware of is how little so many things matter now. What's important and what isn't has shifted.

Lois:

    Images of our swirling energies hit home for me, with all our bubbling energies mixed in together. It certainly will take time to find the 'new normal', the New Life Normal. I do feel helpless and hopeless and very sad, which is quite unlike me.

Richard:

    It was not by good fortune that we all were on this pilgrimage, but all prearranged before we were born—part of our purpose for being here. It only remained to see how many remembered or could be here for the work to be done. Baba's work.

    We are more than the physical body, which is an illusion. What we've done will be recognised when we get home in the hall of records. Much love to all my spiritual co-workers.

Danielle:

    Please know that when I am able to tune in and read some of the emails, it allows me to feel the connections fully. It takes me to the special place that this holds for us in our lives. It is amazing to be able to step away from my daily reality and routines and touch base with the space that we, with God, have created. I feel blessed to have such a place to tune into.

Trail Mix —Kathryn

These U-turns are endless
and even after the Pilgrimage
they continue to spin
in those who, to accomplish all this,
have no sense of direction,
who, without signal for the GPS,
rely wholly and solely upon
faulty print-outs from Google maps,
who seek only batteries for the walkie-talkies,
and who, with the best intentions, always arrive late;
but are still On Time,
who, deprived of rest or regular meals,
still come to dispense the medicine
of forgiveness
without expectation,
to drop a basket of flowers
on a trail of blood and bones,
to affirm the preeminence of human dignity,
and who bravely and whole-heartedly
offer respect in the country of the wounded,
transforming past cruelties into present embrace,
and who trust in this purpose
enough to improvise
in a pattern of work borne by intuition
to their cherished companion,
in Radiant Silence initiated.

Irma:

On November 10, we acquired a handsome, oak roll-top desk with a glassed-in bookcase. I'm rearranging furniture, books and sundries to assimilate this new lovely item into our home. I believe this temporary chaos reflects my internal process of assimilating whatever profound shift I experienced on our pilgrimage. As I sorted things, I found two quotes from Meher Baba:

"The world is now drawing very close to the great upheaval which must precede the breaking of my silence. This upheaval will entail great suffering to humanity, but this suffering will work a profound change of heart and will sweep the world clean for the new and vital phase that must follow."

"During this short period, my Word of words will touch the hearts of all mankind, and spontaneously this divine touch will instill in man the feeling of oneness of all fellow beings. Gradually, in the course of the next seven hundred years, this feeling will supersede the tendency of separateness and rule over the hearts of all, driving away hatred, jealousy and greed that breed suffering, and happiness will reign."

Karl's Baba Dream

I am a passenger in a small red pickup truck headed into Huntington Woods (a hilly suburb of Detroit), on the road home. Ahead of the pickup a girl is walking along, and Baba, who is driving, indicates she needs to hold His hand for just a moment. He slows down alongside her, and I say, "My elder brother thinks you're the sweetest thing. Would you allow Him to hold your hand for just a moment?" She tries to ignore us, but I assure her we are harmless. Rolling her eyes, she comes to the pickup. I have a clear image of her hand in Baba's in front of the dashboard. After a moment Baba lets go and gestures she can go, which she does, still acting huffy. As Baba puts the truck in gear, I say, "Baba, I know you're busy everywhere, running the Universe, so I'd be happy to drive."

"No," He says, *"Driving is my job."*

Irma:

Hmm… U-turns… maybe that's what we've been doing these past weeks…just attached to some old habits…trying to find the right direction.

Jill:

Ah yes, U-turning. Groping in cyberspace with each other, searching the field, staying connected.

Intuitions of Don Stevens

RECALL I HAD A BIG INTUITION IN WHICH I WAS ADVISED I HAD SOMEWHAT CONFUSED THE PURPOSE OF LATER VISITS TO THESE PLACES BY HIS DEVOTEES AS BEING TYPICAL PILGRIMAGES OF WALKING IN THE FOOT-STEPS OF THE MASTER, AND THE CORRECTED PURPOSE WAS TO INTEGRATE THESE VISITORS INTO THE DELIVERY APPARATUS FOR THE SUPPLIES OF SPIRITUAL ENERGY STORED IN THESE PLACES.

Don's intuition is recounted as if he were actually being spoken to. As you read this, remember that Don himself is the 'you' in the narrative of the intuition. The voice of his intuition said this:

"You have felt for some time that beyond Baba's intent that the visits in the future of his devotees to what you call the Power Points he established in India, are not just a following in the footsteps of the Master, as you and others had originally assumed, but something quite different and, in fact, deeply integrated into the functioning of those locations and the energy stored in each. Describing those visits of the devotees as being intended by Baba as forming a part of the actual delivery mechanism of the stored energy, is a very apt wording of Baba's intent, and the manner in which the devotees carried out their visits in January, 2009 was a major step in the direction Baba intended.

However, on several occasions you described the action as being similar to a fire department arriving near the scene of a fire, connecting the fire hose to the fire hydrant provided in the vicinity and having the devotees handle and *point the nozzle* in a direction determined, you suggested, by the spiritual hierarchy."

Don's email dated: Wed, Nov 3, 2010 at 3:37 AM

One should suspect that the new mechanics of the Beads on One String that Baba has set up is a very powerful source of experience which produces unusual and completely unexpected results which can trigger at one stroke a stage of realization that under normal conditions are slowly brought into conscious perception. But here in the intensive atmosphere of group experience developed in a Beads itinerary, time and space are greatly changed and the completely unexpected happens more frequently than not. It is an experience of considerable intensity of decision and on this is built the spiritual structure that normally would require months or more often, of quite some years of duration.

William Donkin:

"A subtle quintessence of love ... pervades everything that Baba does. His physical presence and the brilliance of his leadership have that impossible quality of the philosopher's stone, that by their magic touch, they transmute the base metal of the most commonplace routine into a treasure of loving service.

This is perhaps an ornate way of describing something that is at once so real that one might think it easy to describe quite simply, and so transcendental that the spirit of it eludes the grasp of words.

But this magic, this imponderable something, weaves itself like a golden thread into the fabric of everything that Baba does, and when the factual details of a phase of Baba's life are buried so deep in the ashes of one's mind to be almost forgotten, the memory of this splendid thing is still there."

Don E. Stevens January 14, 1919 - April 26, 2011

The Heartland Pilgrimage was made possible because of Don Stevens, who created the Beads-on-One-String Foundation through a significant financial donation and commitment to the finding of unity and oneness in all of humanity. His love and dedicated work for Meher Baba spanned the globe. Don constantly met with small to large groups throughout the decades, influencing a countless number of people to take an interest in Baba. Through personal contacts the charm of Don's impressive intelligence was only overshadowed by his integrity and genuine love for people. And, unique to these situations, it was done without any sort of religious fervor or campaign. Don handpicked a group of ten people from the UK and the USA to be on the Board of Directors for his Beads-On-One-String Foundation. They were actively sorting out how the foundation would carry out its work at the time of his death, leaving members to unfold those parameters alone. It is to their credit that much has been done since that time.

It was with the active support and encouragement of the Beads-on-One-String Foundation that this Heartland Beads Pilgrimage was realized.

Many thanks to all Heartland Beads for your stories, comments and photographs. Jai Meher Baba.

Irma Sheppard, Editor

Karl Moeller, Layoutwalla

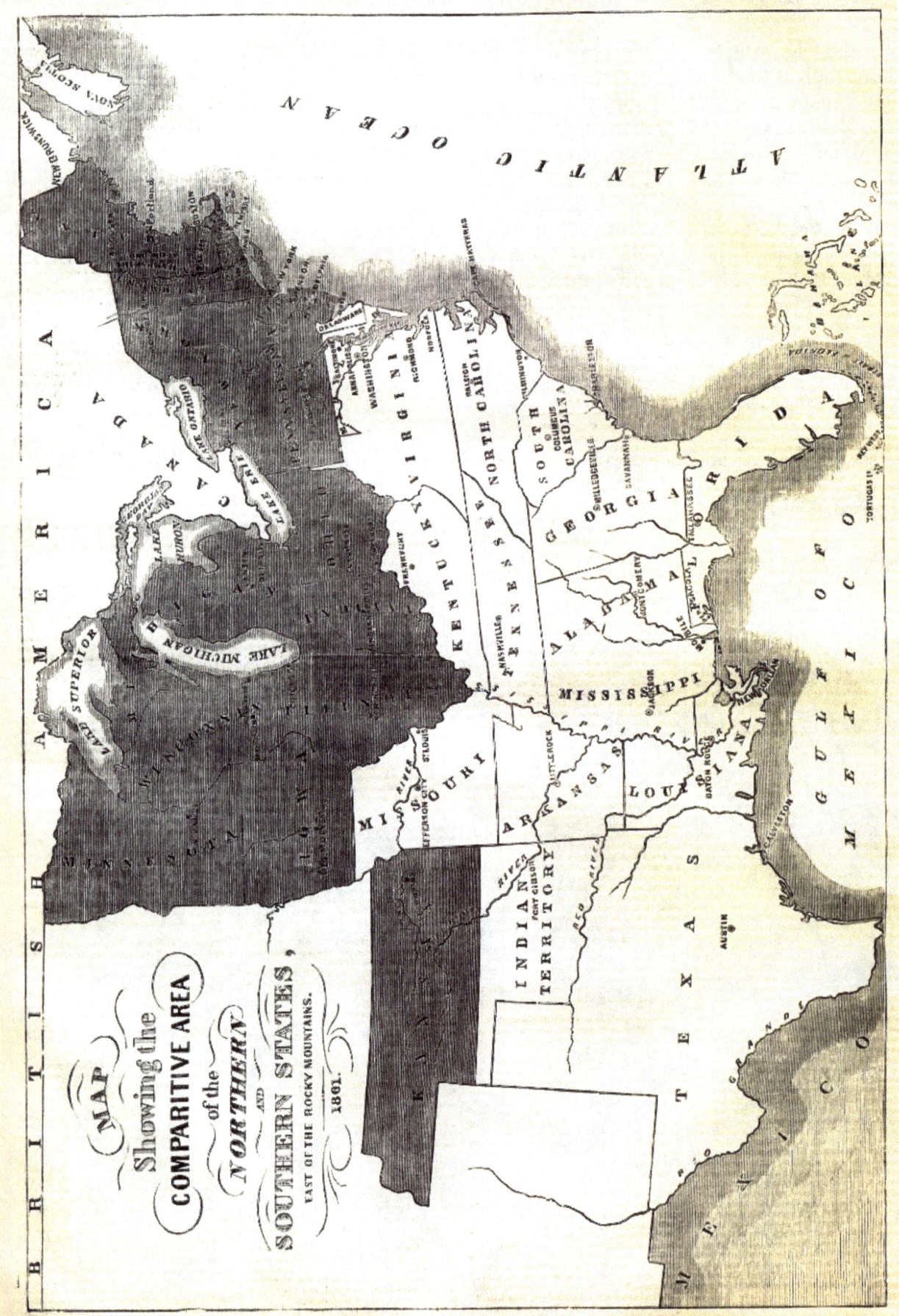

www.ingramcontent.com/pod-product-compliance
Lightning Source LLC
Chambersburg PA
CBHW080351170426
43194CB00014B/2750